STARTING · WITH · SCIENCE
SOLIDS, LIQUIDS AND GASES

THE · ONTARIO · SCIENCE · CENTRE

PHOTOGRAPHS BY RAY BOUDREAU

Heinemann Children's Reference and Kids Can Press Ltd acknowledge with appreciation the assistance of the Canada Council, the Ontario Arts Council and Gavin Barrett in the production of this book.

First published in Canada in 1995 by Kids Can Press Ltd,
29 Birch Avenue, Toronto, Ontario, Canada, M4V 1E2.
This edition published in Great Britain in 1997 by
Heinemann Children's Reference, an imprint of Heinemann Educational Publishers, Halley Court, Jordan Hill, Oxford, OX2 8EJ.

MADRID ATHENS PARIS FLORENCE PORTSMOUTH NH CHICAGO
SAO PAULO SINGAPORE TOKYO MELBOURNE AUCKLAND
IBADAN GABORONE JOHANNESBURG KAMPALA NAIROBI

Text copyright © 1995 by The Ontario Science Centre
Photographs copyright © 1995 by Ray Boudreau
All rights reserved. No part of this publication may be reproduced, stored in a retrieval system, or transmitted, in any form or by any means, electronic, mechanical, photocopying, recording, or otherwise, without the prior permission of the copyright holders or a licence permitting restricted copying in the United Kingdom, issued by the Copyright Licensing Agency Ltd, 90 Tottenham Court Rd, London W1P 9HE.

British Library Cataloguing in Publication Data
A catalogue record for this book is available from the British Library.

ISBN 0 431 01615 1 (hardback) 0 431 01620 8 (paperback)

PLEASE READ THIS
For some of the activities in this book you will need to use tools and materials, such as scissors or knife, and hot water. Be very careful when you are using them, and always make sure an adult is there to help you. Always wash your hands when doing any of the activities that use foodstuffs.

Neither the Publishers nor the Author shall be liable for any damage which may be caused or sustained as a result of the conduct of any of the activities in this book, from not specifically following instructions or conducting the activities without proper supervision, or from ignoring the cautions contained in the text.

Written by Louise Oborne and Carol Gold
Edited by Valerie Wyatt and Alex Gray
Designed by James Ireland/Peter Enneson
Printed in Hong Kong.

Table of contents

Balloon blow-up 4	Strong air 20
Rock candy 6	Summer frost 22
Magnet power! 8	Indoor rain 24
Ice fishing 10	Raisin race 26
Ice cream dream 12	Ooblik 28
Water wonder 14	For parents and teachers 30
Soap boat 16	Words to know 31
Empty glass trick 18	Index..32

Balloon blow-up

You can blow up a balloon with your mouth. But here's a way to blow one up without any huffing and puffing.

You will need:
- a balloon
- a small funnel
- a spoon
- baking soda
- vinegar
- a small juice or drinks bottle

What to do:
1. Stretch the balloon, so that it will be easy to blow up.
2. Use the funnel to put two large spoonfuls of baking soda into the balloon.
3. Half fill the bottle with vinegar.
4. Stretch the neck of the balloon over the neck of the bottle. (You should ask an adult to help you with this.) Don't let any baking soda fall into the bottle.
5. Ready to blow up the balloon? Hold the balloon up so that all the baking soda falls into the vinegar in the bottle.

What's happening?
When the baking soda (a solid) and vinegar (a liquid) mixed, they produced a gas called carbon dioxide. The gas took up more room than there was in the bottle, so some of it flowed into the balloon and blew it up.

Solids, liquids and gases
Everything in the whole world is made of tiny bits called molecules. How close together the molecules are and how they move is different in solids, liquids and gases. Get some friends together and act like a solid, liquid or gas.

Hold hands and stand as close together as you can — really squeeze together — and stay very still. You are acting like the molecules in a solid.

Still holding hands, spread out so you can move. Sway and walk so the group forms different shapes. Now you are acting like the molecules in a liquid.

Let go of your hands and spread out. Run around. Bump *gently* into one another. Now you are acting like the molecules in a gas.

Rock candy

What's hard as a rock and sweet as candy? Rock candy! Ask an adult to help you mix a solid with a liquid to make some rock candy.

You will need:
- a small saucepan
- 250 ml (1 cup) water
- 375 ml (1½ cups) sugar, or more
- a wooden spoon
- a plastic jar
- a pencil
- a piece of clean cotton string

What to do:
1. Ask an adult to boil the water in the saucepan and remove it from the stove.
2. Add the sugar to the water and stir. (Ask an adult to help you with this step, too. The water is very hot.)
3. When all the sugar disappears, stir in more. Keep adding a little at a time until you can see sugar floating in the water.
4. Let the sugar water cool a little. Then pour it into the jar.
5. Tie the cotton string around the pencil. Rub some sugar into the string, so that a few grains stick to it.
6. Drop the free end of the string into the sugary water. Rest the pencil on the rim of the jar.
7. Put the jar in a cool place, then leave it to stand without moving it.
8. Wait a few days, then gently pull the string from the water. Taste the solid that clings to the string.

What's happening?
The sugar didn't really disappear. Each tiny piece of sugar broke into smaller and smaller bits and spread out in the water. This is called dissolving. Because the water was warm, its molecules were spread far apart. There was room for the little bits of sugar to fit between the molecules. When the water cooled, its molecules moved close together again and squeezed the sugar out. The little bits of sugar stuck to the sugar already on the string and formed large chunks.

What is a solid?
Solids are hard. They don't change shape easily. The molecules in a solid are packed together tightly and don't move around.

Magnet power!

Drive a car without an engine. There's no magic to it — just magnets.

You will need:
- paper
- coloured markers or crayons
- scissors
- sticky tape
- a metal paper clip
- a large piece of light cardboard
- a magnet (a small fridge magnet might not be strong enough to work)

What to do:

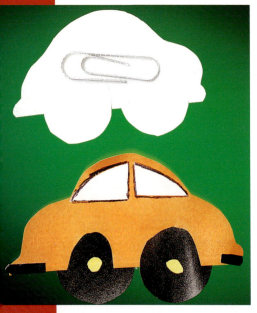

1. On the paper, draw a car the size shown here.
2. Ask an adult to cut out the car. Colour the car if you wish.
3. Tape the paper clip to the back of the cut-out car.
4. Draw roads on the piece of cardboard. Make sure the roads are wide enough for your car. Add some houses, shops and trees.
5. Put the car on one of the roads. Hold the magnet beneath the cardboard, right under the car. Move the magnet to move the car. Can you steer it along the roads?

What's happening?
A magnet is a special kind of solid that pulls metal objects towards it. Why? Because a magnet has an invisible force field that many metal objects just can't help following. Your car moved because the metal paper clip taped to it was following the magnet's force field.

Sticking together
Collect some solids, including a penny, a nail, a ball of paper, a pencil rubber and a button. Try picking up each with the magnet. Put the solids you can pick up in one pile and the ones you can't in another. What's different about the two piles?

Ice fishing

Can you lift an ice cube out of a glass of water with a piece of string? No knots allowed! Sounds impossible? Here's how.

You will need:
- a small ice cube
- a jar of cold water
- a piece of string about 15 cm long
- salt

What to do:
1. Put the ice cube into the jar of water. Wait until it stops bobbing.
2. Carefully lay one end of the string across the top of the ice cube.
3. Sprinkle some salt over the string where it touches the ice.
4. Slowly count to 10, then gently lift the string. Wow! You've caught an ice cube. But how?
(If the ice cube falls, start all over with a fresh ice cube and clean water.)

What's happening?
When you sprinkled salt onto the ice cube, the ice cube melted a bit. A little pool of water formed on the top of the ice cube and the string sank into it. Then the pool of water froze, trapping the string.

What is melting?

The molecules in a solid are close together and don't move. The molecules in a liquid are spread out and can move. When a solid gets warm enough, the molecules start to move and get farther apart. The solid starts to turn into a liquid. This is called melting.

Ice cream dream

Stir up a batch of delicious old-fashioned ice cream ready to eat — and discover how you can change a liquid into a solid at the same time!

You will need:
- 125 ml (½ cup) cold whipping cream
- 25 ml (2 tablespoons) white sugar
- a drop of vanilla flavouring
- a measuring jug
- a large foam or plastic cup, 300–350 ml
- finely crushed ice
- 60 ml (4 tablespoons) salt
- 2 plastic stirring sticks or spoons
- a small paper cup, about 150 ml

What to do:
1. Mix the cream, sugar and vanilla together in the measuring jug. Chill the mixture in the fridge.
2. Fill the larger foam cup about one-third full with ice.
3. Add the salt to the ice and stir. (Mark the stirring stick so you won't use it by mistake in the ice cream mixture you will want to eat.)

4. Pour enough cream and sugar mixture from the measuring jug to fill the paper cup three-quarters full.

5. Make a hole in the icy slush in the foam cup big enough for the paper cup. Add more ice mixed with salt around the paper cup. Don't let the salty mixture get into the cream mixture!

6. Stir the cream mixture quickly with a clean stick. You will have to stir for quite a while, so you may want help.

7. As you stir, scrape around the bottom and sides of the paper cup to loosen any frozen bits. Stop from time to time to let the ice cream mixture harden. In about 20 minutes the ice cream will be ready.

What's happening?
You started out with a liquid mixture of cream and sugar. The crushed ice cooled the liquid into a solid as you stirred.

What is freezing?
Liquids turn into solids when they get very cold. Why? Because the molecules huddle closer together and stop moving. This is called freezing.

Water wonder

Look at the three containers. Which one has the most water? Read on to find out.

You will need:
- 3 clear containers of different sizes and shapes (for example, a glass, a bowl and a salad dressing bottle)
- 2 measuring cups
- water
- food colouring
- a friend

What to do:
1. Before your friend arrives, fill each container with 250 ml (1 cup) of water.
2. Stir a few drops of food colouring into each container.
3. Line the containers up on a table. Ask your friend to guess which has the most water and which has the least.
4. Empty the container your friend says has the most water into one of the measuring cups. Pour the water from the container with the 'least' water into the other cup. Is your friend surprised?

What's happening?
When you poured water into the containers, it spread out inside. If you have a small container, the water may fill it up. If the container is large, the water may only cover the bottom. So the small container may *appear* to have more water than the large one.

What is a liquid?
The molecules in a liquid are loosely connected and can move around to fill whatever space they are in.

Soap boat

Next time you fill up a bath or paddling pool, try sending a power boat zooming through the water. And you can use shampoo or washing up liquid for fuel!

You will need:
- a pencil
- scissors
- a piece of cardboard with a shiny surface (a piece of empty cereal box works well)
- a bath tub or paddling pool
- shampoo or washing up liquid

What to do:

1. Draw a boat the size of your hand on a piece of shiny cardboard.
2. Cut out the boat shape. Be sure to cut out a notch at the back. Younger children should ask an adult to help them.
3. Put water in a bath tub or paddling pool. Wait until the water is still, then gently rest the cardboard boat on the surface with the shiny side down.
4. Put a small drop of shampoo into the notch at the back of the boat. Watch it go! Add another drop of shampoo when your boat slows down. How long can you keep your boat going?

What's happening?

Water molecules like to stick together. They hold on to one another and form a kind of 'skin' over the water's surface. You can't see or feel this 'skin', which is called surface tension. Shampoo or washing up liquid 'unzips' this skin. The boat moves along like the pull on a clothes zip.

Empty glass trick

Is an empty glass really empty? If you said 'yes', you're in for a surprise…

You will need:
- a paper towel
- a tumbler

What to do:
1. Stuff the paper towel tightly into the bottom of the tumbler. It should stay there even when you hold the tumbler upside down.
2. Fill a sink with water.
3. Turn the tumbler upside down. Hold the tumbler very straight and plunge it into the water.
4. Slowly count to 10. Lift the tumbler out of the water without tipping it.
5. Pull the paper towel out of the tumbler. Is the paper still dry?

What's happening?
The paper towel stayed dry because the water couldn't get into the tumbler. Why not? Because the tumbler was already full of air!

A huff 'n puff trick
Try this trick on your friends. Push a deflated balloon into a large plastic drink bottle. Stretch the open end of the balloon back over the bottle's mouth. Challenge a friend to blow up the balloon. Why won't it work?

What is a gas?
Your bottle and tumbler are full of air — which is a mixture of gases. Smell the gases in the air. Stick out your tongue and taste them. Most gases don't have a smell or a taste, and most are invisible. But we know they are around us because they take up space, just as the air in your bottle and tumbler does.

Strong air

Turn a tumbler of water upside down and the water will pour out. Or will it? Try this to find out.

You will need:
- a tumbler half filled with water
- a piece of stiff, flat cardboard

What to do:
1. Put the cardboard over the top of the tumbler.
2. Hold the cardboard tight against the rim of the tumbler.
3. Turn the tumbler upside down, over a sink, while holding the cardboard in place. Keep the tumbler facing down.
4. Take your hand away from the cardboard. Surprised?

What's happening?
Air pushes up, down and sideways on everything it touches. This pushing power is called air pressure. The air outside the tumbler pushed up on the cardboard more than the water and air inside the tumbler pushed down. This kept the water from falling into the sink.

Summer frost

Frost in summer? Sounds impossible? Try this and see for yourself!

You will need:
- Epsom salts (available from chemists)
- 50 ml (¼ cup) very hot water
- a clear pie plate or baking dish

What to do:
1. Ask an adult to help you pour a spoonful of Epsom salts into the hot water. Stir until the salts disappear.
2. Pour a thin layer of the salt water into the glass dish.
3. Set the dish outside in the sun or in a warm place and leave it for an hour. Where did the frost come from?

What's happening?
You didn't make real frost. You made a sparkling pattern that looked like frost. How? The Epsom salts separated into tiny pieces that fit in between the water molecules. As the water evaporated, the little pieces of salt were pushed back together. They stuck to tiny bumps and scratches in the glass. The pieces can only fit together in certain ways. This produces a pattern that looks like frost.

What is evaporation?
As the water warmed up, it turned into a gas called 'water vapour' and floated away in the air. This change from a liquid to a gas is called evaporation. However, the salt did not evaporate — it was left behind on the bottom of the dish.

Indoor rain

Have you ever been stuck inside on a rainy day? Where does all that rain come from? Try making some rain in your own kitchen to find out.

You will need:
- a large metal spoon or soup ladle
- a kettle one-quarter filled with water
- oven gloves

What to do:
1. Put the spoon into the freezer to cool it. Leave it there until it's ice cold.
2. Ask an adult to boil water in the kettle.
3. When the water is boiling, put on your oven gloves and remove the spoon from the freezer.
4. With the oven gloves on, hold the cold spoon in the cloud of steam coming from the kettle's spout. In a few seconds you'll see 'rain' falling from the bottom of the spoon.

What's happening?
When the cloud of air and water vapour touched the spoon, it cooled suddenly. Cooling makes the molecules of air in the cloud scrunch closer together, which pushes out the water. This is called condensation. The water falls. Presto! Indoor rain.

Outdoor rain
When the sun warms up the water in rivers, lakes, oceans and puddles, some of the water evaporates. The water vapour rises into the sky and forms a cloud. Cold air up in the sky can't hold as much water as warm air can. So the water vapour cools and turns into droplets of water. Thousands of droplets form a raindrop, which then falls from the cloud. It's time to get out your umbrella!

What is condensation?

When warm, moist air meets a cool surface, tiny droplets of water form. We call this condensation. Try breathing on a cold window. The water in your warm breath condenses on the cold window.

Raisin race

Open a bottle of fizzy drink and you'll hear a fizz and see bubbles. There is a gas dissolved in the liquid! You can use the gas to give some raisins a ride.

You will need:
- a clear plastic tumbler
- lemonade or other clear fizzy drink
- several raisins
- a spoon

What to do:
1. Carefully pour the lemonade into the tumbler. If you tip the tumbler and pour the lemonade gently down the side, you will keep more of the fizz in the liquid.
2. Drop two raisins into the lemonade. Watch them race up and down.
3. Use the spoon to remove the raisins. Squeeze one of them to flatten it. Now drop both of the raisins back into the lemonade. Does one raisin go up and down faster than the other?
4. You can also put a bunch of raisins into the lemonade and watch them race!

What's happening?
The raisins rise on a bubble cloud. Where do the bubbles come from? Fizzy drinks have a gas called carbon dioxide dissolved in them. At the factory, a machine pumps the gas into the drink, then the lid is sealed. When you open the drink, the hiss you hear is the gas starting to escape.

As the gas comes out of the spaces between the molecules of liquid, it sticks to the raisins. When there are lots of bubbles, they lift the raisin to the surface. There the bubbles break and the raisin sinks again.

Ooblik

Make some ooblik and you'll discover that things aren't always what they seem. Is this melt-in-your-hand marvel a liquid — or a solid?

You will need:
- 2 or 3 sheets of newspaper
- a box of corn flour
- a small cake tin
- a jug of water (add some food colouring, if you wish)
- a spoon

What to do:
1. Spread the newspaper out on a table.
2. Put some corn flour into the pan and add some of the water. Stir.
3. Keep adding water and stirring until the mixture is as thick as mayonnaise. You've made ooblik. Make more ooblik until you have a layer 1 cm deep.
4. Lift up a spoonful of ooblik and pour it back into the pan. Does it pour out easily?
5. Slap the pan of ooblik with the flat of your hand. Does any splash out?
6. Scoop up a handful of ooblik. Roll it around between your hands to make a ball. When you think you've made a ball, lift your top hand up. What happens? **Don't pour the ooblik down the drain.** Scrape it into the dustbin.

What's happening?
Corn flour is made of millions of tiny particles. When you add water to the flour, the particles float freely, evenly spaced apart.

Imagine the floating starch particles are like people going through a doorway. If everyone walks in an evenly spaced line, the people pass through easily. But if everyone tries to push through at once, the group gets jammed in the doorway.

The same thing happens to ooblik. When you move the ooblik mixture slowly or gently, when you stir it or pour it, the flour particles can slide easily past one another. The mixture acts like a liquid. When you try to move the mixture quickly or push it hard, such as slapping it or squeezing it, the flour particles get pushed together and the mixture acts just like a solid.

For parents and teachers

Experimenting is a good way to introduce young children to principles of science. The activities in this book are designed to show that matter is everywhere, that matter comes in three forms (solid, liquid or gas) and that these forms can be changed by factors such as temperature or pressure. Here are some ideas to extend the activities in the book. These questions invite children to develop theories and test them through open-ended experimentation.

Balloon blow-up
What is a solid? A liquid? A gas? Have a hunt around your house or school and list all the solids, liquids and gases you can find there.

Rock candy
What other solids dissolve when placed in a liquid? Fill several tumblers with water and put a different solid into each. Try salt, chocolate drink powder, rice, instant coffee, coffee beans. Which solids dissolve? How are they similar?

Magnet power!
In most solids, molecules are aligned in random directions. In a magnet, all the molecules are lined up in the same direction. To make a simple magnet, rub a metal paper clip in one direction along a magnet about 50 times. Can your paper clip pick up other paper clips or objects?

Ice fishing and Ice cream dream
Why was salt used in these two experiments? Salt lowers the freezing point of water. When salt mixed with the wet surface of the ice, the resulting salt water wasn't cold enough to stay frozen. In the process of melting, it actually loses heat and gets even colder. Try putting a thermometer into a glass of ice and adding salt. Does the temperature drop?

Water wonder
Do different liquids move in different ways? Pour water from one glass into another. How long does it take? Test the pouring time of other liquids, such as cooking oil, washing up liquid and syrup. The size of the molecules and how much they cling together (their 'viscosity') determine the speeds at which they flow.

Soap boat
Fill a glass with water. Does the water bulge over the top? The molecules of water cling together, almost like a 'skin' over the surface, keeping the water from spilling over. This is called 'surface tension'.

Empty glass trick
Which takes up more space — warm air or cool air? Blow up a balloon then deflate it. Put the mouth of the balloon over the neck of an empty bottle. Set the bottle in a pan of hot water. Wait for a few minutes. What happens to the balloon? Replace the hot water with ice. What happens to the balloon now?

Strong air
Try the same experiment using a piece of mesh instead of cardboard. Is the air pressure still strong enough to keep the water in the tumbler?

Summer frost
Hold an evaporation race! Ask a child to make a water droplet evaporate. Try blowing on it, fanning it, or drying it with a hair dryer or lamp. Which method is fastest? Why?

Indoor rain
Where else does water condense? Put a small potted plant into a plastic bag and seal it. Water evaporates from the plant's leaves and condenses on the bag.

Raisin race
Fizzy drink contains gas. What other foods contain gases? Make some fairy cakes or muffins. The holes inside are caused by carbon dioxide that was formed when baking soda was combined with acidic ingredients in the mixture and heated. Do other foods have these gas holes?

Ooblik
What helps a liquid change to a solid? Try gently heating some ooblik. In a saucepan mix 250 ml (1 cup) corn starch, 500 ml (2 cups) baking soda and 375 ml (1½ cups) water. Cook until clumps form, pour into a bowl, cover with a damp cloth and cool. Has the ooblik changed? Use it like clay.

Words to know

air: a mixture of gases, mainly nitrogen and oxygen

air pressure: the force that air places on anything it touches

condensation: a process in which a gas changes to a liquid

dissolve: to change a substance by mixing it into a liquid

evaporation: a process in which a liquid changes to a gas

freeze: to change a liquid to a solid by cooling it

gas: a form of matter whose molecules are not connected to one another and move randomly in space. Oxygen is a gas.

liquid: a form of matter that can flow freely and take on the shape of its container. Water is a liquid.

matter: any substance that takes up space and has weight. Matter has different forms — it can be a solid, a liquid or a gas.

melt: to change a solid to a liquid by heating it

molecule: the tiniest particle into which a substance can be broken without changing it chemically. All matter is made up of molecules.

solid: a form of matter that has a rigid shape. A rock is a solid.

Index

air 18, 19, 20, 22, 24, 25
air pressure 20

balloons 4, 5, 19
breath 25

carbon dioxide 5, 26
clouds 24
condensation 24, 25

dissolving 6, 26
dust 24

evaporation 22, 24

fizzy drinks 26
freezing 10, 13

gases 5, 19, 22, 26. *See also* air, carbon dioxide

ice cubes 10

liquids 5, 6, 11, 12, 13, 14, 22, 26, 28

magnets 8
melting 10, 11
metals 8
molecules 5, 6, 7, 11, 13, 14, 17, 24, 26

rain 24

solids 5, 6, 7, 8, 11, 12, 13, 28
sun 24
surface tension 17, 30

water vapour 22
water's skin. *See* surface tension